CONTENTS

Coping with loss 4

Living with guilt — 6
During her teens, Liana had a difficult relationship with her mother and feels long-lasting guilt at not spending more time with her mother when she was dying of cancer.

Losing a brother — 10
Dan was a teenager when his elder brother Rory died of cancer. Dan felt he had to take on the role of caring for the rest of the family.

Keeping a friend in mind — 14
Laura and her friends found that grieving together helped them.

Caring for my mother — 16
Amelia cared for her mother at home when she was dying of cancer.

Holding on to memories — 20
Hugo, 14, misses his granddad but holds on to the happy memories.

Coping with a tragic death — 22
Maya lost her father when she was 13 and her mother died in an horrific road incident eight months ago.

Hearing from abroad — 26
While he was trekking in Nepal, David heard that a very close friend had died suddenly of meningitis.

Feeling betrayed — 28
Charlie felt betrayed by her close uncle's death and did not know how to deal with the grief.

Glossary 30

Further information 31

Index and Talking Points 32

COPING WITH LOSS

The experience of losing a loved one is surprisingly common for young people. Around 92% of people suffer the loss of a parent, grandparent, relative, sibling, classmate or treasured pet, before the age of 16. The reaction to death depends not only on the importance and closeness of the person who died but also on the personality of the young person. Young people react in different ways, and not always as adults might expect.

Living in denial

Denial is a way some people, and young children especially, may attempt to cope. They refuse to accept the reality of what has happened and will choose not to talk about it. Or they might suddenly become very difficult and confrontational; aggression and even violence may be ways anger, pain and impotence are displayed.

Guilt

Guilt can add to the pain. Children who feel they have not been good enough to the deceased person or regret something said or done can suffer quite disproportionate guilt. Sometimes they feel they have contributed to the bereavement.

Worry

Being forced to confront mortality is a loss of innocence – it can make a young person suddenly very anxious about the future; they may be filled with fearful wondering about who will care for them from now on (in the case of a parental loss), or even be concerned about their own mortality.

Losing 'yourself'

After a bereavement young people in particular may lose self-confidence and their sense of their own identity or self. The child may see his or her role in the family altered. In due course bereavement can mean goals and dreams have to be re-evaluated and re-structured. Young people may question their faith and feel they may never have a sense of joy again.

Supporting a bereaved person

Support, comfort and understanding from family, friends and teachers is very important even if a young person appears not to want or need these things. However, classmates, family friends, neighbours, teachers, school friends and boyfriends or girlfriends can often feel hopelessly at a loss: clumsy, tongue-tied and frightened of intruding when they are not wanted.

But talking about the dead person and sharing memories is important, so don't feel you are being insensitive. Not talking about them can feel to the young person as though the dead person is no longer part of what matters. It is important to recognise that the tragedy can feel all-engulfing, so avoid observations such as "it could have been worse"; "it's not as bad as ...".

When more support is needed

If young people can get enough help and support most will not need professional help. But if a child goes on being very distressed or disturbing in their behaviour contact a child bereavement organisation, such as the Child Bereavement Trust, or your doctor.

This book

Many people find that hearing the stories of others who have suffered the death of a loved one is helpful. The young people who have offered their experiences for this book describe the process of going through the shock and realisation; how sharing grief with peers can be helpful. Many are honest about how guilt – often exaggerated and misplaced – is a powerful emotion. And they talk about how it is possible to move forward. As the Child Bereavement Trust points out, "It does not matter what age you are when someone important in your life dies or leaves you. It's probably not possible to ever totally prepare a young person for the death of someone important in their lives." Hopefully the stories in this book will help, if only in some small way.

TYPICAL BEREAVEMENT REACTIONS

YOUNG CHILDREN
Young children find it very difficult to understand the finality of death, but by age 11 they know death is final and that it can happen to them.

Common reactions to bereavement are:

• Crying, aggression, longing, resentment, isolation and withdrawal, sleep disturbance, suppressed emotions, concern about their own physical health, difficulties with school work.

TEENAGERS
Teenagers struggling towards independence may be more afraid of exposing feelings.

Common reactions to bereavement are:

• Numbing, anger, resentment, anxiety, guilt, sense of increased responsibility, risk-taking and acting-out behaviour, avoidance of feelings, appetite and sleep changes, difficulties with school work, apathy.

Long-term problems
Around 5–10% of children and teens are likely to suffer adjustment problems in the first year after the loss. Depression is the commonest of these. Causes for concern if they go on beyond the first year are:

• Long-term denial, appetite and weight loss, sleep disturbance, hopelessness and profound emptiness, inability to respond to comfort and rejection of support, destructive outbursts, prolonged physical complaints, inappropriate or illegal behaviour, repeated talk of wanting to be dead.

LIVING WITH GUILT

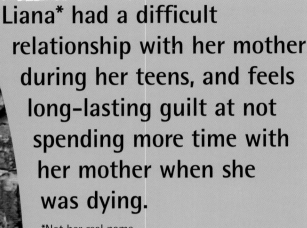

Liana* had a difficult relationship with her mother during her teens, and feels long-lasting guilt at not spending more time with her mother when she was dying.

*Not her real name.

Q Were you living at home when your mother became ill?

No. It was three years ago. I had just started a teaching job about 160 kilometres from home and I was moving into a flat with a friend. I wasn't really aware of what was going on with Mum. Then one day I got a call from Dad saying she had lung cancer. I rushed home but it was awkward because my mother was a very private person and didn't want my brother and me to make a fuss.

" ... one day I got a call from Dad saying [Mum] had lung cancer."

TALKING ABOUT
MYSELF

LOSING A LOVED ONE

Interviews by Angela Neustatter
Photographs by Laurence Cendrowicz

W
FRANKLIN WATTS
LONDON•SYDNEY

First published in 2008 by Franklin Watts

Franklin Watts,
338 Euston Road,
London, NW1 3BH

Franklin Watts Australia,
Level 17/207 Kent Street,
Sydney, NSW 2000

Series editor: Sarah Peutrill
Art Director: Jonathan Hair
Design: Elaine Wilkinson
Additional research by: Charlotte Wormald
Panels written by: Sarah Ridley
Photographs: Laurence Cendrowicz (unless otherwise stated)

The Author and Publisher would like to thank the interviewees for their
contributions to this book.

Picture credits: Galina Barskaya/Shutterstock: 9. James Boulette/istockphoto: 13.
Alistair Cotton/Shutterstock: 18. Olly Hoeben: 6, 7, 10, 12, 13, 14.
MalibuBooks/Shutterstock: 23. Dick Stada/Shutterstock: 27. Vasil
Vasilev/Shutterstock: 29. Every attempt has been made to clear copyright. Should
there be any inadvertent omission please apply to the publisher for rectification.

Dewey number: 306.88

ISBN: 978 0 7496 7708 4

Printed in China

Franklin Watts is a division of Hachette Children's Books,
an Hachette Livre UK company.

Q Did you change your life?

No I didn't and I feel guilty every day about that. I don't think I really registered how ill she was and I didn't make much effort to help. I was still behaving in my nasty adolescent way. Mum and I had had a difficult relationship when I was a teenager because I opposed her a lot and didn't want to be the way she wanted me to be. I think I was very selfish. And when she was ill I didn't even go home that often at weekends, and that is terrible because she only lived for six more months.

Q How did your father cope?

I was aware he seemed very stressed. He was working full time then sitting up through the night with Mum. She didn't want to go to sleep because then she woke up and remembered she was ill. Luckily my brother was living at home to help.

Q What happened then?

Mum died in March. I had gone home the weekend before and she was in bed all weekend but even so I didn't realise how ill she was. I stayed up all Saturday evening and into the early hours talking with Mum and I am so, so glad I did that. Then on the Sunday I had to leave because of work and I had this abnormal feeling. I didn't want to go. Mum seemed very sad and I suppose she realised she might not see me again. But she didn't say anything.

Q How did you find out?

The phone rang on the Thursday at breakfast time and it was Dad. He couldn't speak then he just managed to get the words out. Afterwards I cried because of shock but the awful thing was I didn't feel anything, just numb. ▶

"I cried because of the shock but the awful thing was I didn't feel anything, just numb."

Bury College
Woodbury LRC

7

Q What happened then?

I went home and Mum was laid out upstairs. I didn't want to go and see her, but I felt I'd regret it if I didn't. Seeing her like that frightened me. The undertakers came to take the body and Dad went into the garden and I knew how upset he was, but there was nothing I could do. For three or four days after that we all just stayed in the house.

DEALING WITH GUILT

Guilt is just one of the emotions that people can feel when they have lost someone close to them. Could they have done more? Why did they say that? Why weren't they there? Why didn't they behave more kindly towards that person? Could they have prevented the death? The list is endless. These feelings are natural and are part of the grieving process.

Some people find it helps to talk over their guilt with their family or friends. Others make themselves think of happy times with that person, rather than focusing on bad times, or things that were said. However guilty you might feel, like the other emotions of bereavement, in time the guilt will fade and you will come to cope with it.

"For three or four days after that we all just stayed in the house."

Q How did you cope with the funeral?

That was easier than I expected. I found the cremation upsetting, but it was a busy day with Mum's friends, and family friends there. I'd organised the flowers as something I could do for Mum. After this was over time just seemed to exist. I chose to stay home because I didn't want to leave Dad.

Q Did you grieve a lot?

That was the scary thing I didn't. I found myself crying sometimes but really I felt nothing for about six months. It was as though I were emptied out. When I went home it hit me because I felt Mum's presence there. It was a very unreal, surreal time. For a while I had a relationship with a boy I really liked, but I don't think he could cope with my neediness so he ended it.

Q And now, three years later, do you feel you have found a way to move on?

Not really. But I see my personality has totally changed. I feel very depressed and my moods go up and down a lot. Sometimes everything is very black. I don't think I am as nice a person as I was. I can be very negative and self-pitying.

"I train for marathons and that feels good."

Have you thought of getting help?

Friends have suggested I should talk to someone professional about it and I think perhaps that is what I should do. I really want to be able to remember Mum in a happy way and not feel so guilty.

Do you enjoy yourself at all?

There are times when I go out with close friends for drinks and a meal and I am aware of enjoying myself. I train for marathons and that feels good. The thing I find very hard indeed is if I'm alone at a weekend with nothing planned. I can't be on my own. I sit and cry and I get hysterical. I believe things will get better but I don't know when. ∎

LOSING A BROTHER

Dan was a teenager when his elder brother Rory died of cancer aged 19. Dan felt he had to take on the role of caring for the rest of the family.

Q How did you react when you learnt that your brother had cancer?

Of course it was a shock but Rory seemed to get better and I assumed that was it. Then, a year later, his cancer came back. But I convinced myself he would recover again and I spent a lot of time during his illness away. When I went home at Christmas the doctors told us he could get better and we all clung to this although, looking back, I can see he was so sick it really wasn't possible. But Rory never spoke to me about his cancer.

" ... the doctors told us he could get better and we all clung to this ... I can see he was so sick it really wasn't possible."

What happened then?

I got a phone call from his girlfriend saying he hadn't got much time. I had to face reality. I went home and that was the hardest week of my life because Rory was dying before our eyes.

What did you do during this time?

I kept very busy organising friends to come and see Rory and say goodbye. I felt I had to cope and be strong for my parents and my two younger brothers. As a family there was an unspoken agreement that we didn't want to be melancholy around Rory. Even when we sat with him as he died we were being upbeat talking to him.

How important was it for you to be there when he died?

It was very important for us and for Rory I think. But the real grief didn't kick in then. Not for ages.

Did your role in the family change now you were the eldest?

Very quickly I felt I had to look after everyone in the family, but especially my brothers. They were in shock and angry. One tried to buy a lot of drugs but I put a stop to that. After this they went into denial and didn't appear to feel much at all. I knew they really needed support to face the fact, as I had to, that the unthinkable had happened. ▶

BEREAVEMENT AND DEPRESSION

The intensely sad feelings that many people experience after losing someone close are completely natural but they can be difficult to shake off. If a bereaved person continues to feel very low and shows little interest in work, friendships, family or hobbies over a period of weeks and months, he or she may be suffering depression.

WHAT TO DO?
Talking to someone is a good start, whether it is a friend, teacher or health professional. Doctors, nurses or counsellors are all trained to give good advice on how to diagnose depression, and recover from it. Some people may need medicinal drugs, therapy or counselling to come to terms with their loss. For many it is simply a matter of time.

"I was very lethargic. I broke up with my girlfriend. It was difficult to get out of bed in the morning."

So how was the family?

We held together very well for the first year. We were close. We all went on holiday together even though my parents hadn't been getting on, and we had a fantastic, rather unreal, week. I think we got a lot of power, as a family, from having helped Rory to die the best way we could.

How was the time after this?

I was very lethargic. I broke up with my girlfriend. It was difficult to get out of bed in the morning. So I went to see a counsellor but that was disastrous. He ended up crying with me when I told what had happened. In fact I got into another relationship and thought the girl was the love of my life but it didn't last and I slipped back into depression. I found myself thinking about Rory every day. He and I had been very close and would have been the best of friends now.

Did your behaviour change?

I started crying often but the good thing was I talked to Mum a lot and she suggested practical things for me to do, rather than talking about Rory all the time. But things were made much harder by Mum and Dad going through a divorce and there were a lot of angry rows. I felt I had to protect my brothers from this and I became the go-between for my parents which was a nightmare. Looking back it was a truly

THE GRIEVING PROCESS

Grief will affect everyone at some time in their life and there is no one way to cope with losing someone close to you. Many people feel completely numb at first. Other people feel weighed down by sadness, weep all the time and can only think of their loss. Some feel anger or guilt. They may even feel guilty that they are still alive. Through it all grief can be physically exhausting, especially if the bereaved person is finding it difficult to sleep. It can take someone weeks, months or years to come to terms with what has happened.

GETTING BACK TO NORMAL
Going back to school or work helps some people to deal with their grief. If they go about their normal lives, they are busy and they find that gradually they come to cope with their loss. Other people feel they need some time to rest and think before they return to the normal world of school, college or work. Both are completely acceptable ways to come through grief.

difficult time. I ran the home, cooked for everyone who was there and I gave my brothers money when they needed it because I had got a job. I wanted them to see that I was there and stable. When I wasn't at home I phoned them a lot.

> "lacrosse particularly ... really lifted my mood when things were tough in my head."

Q And now, eight years on?

Well I took up sport again. Getting myself to do sport, lacrosse particularly because I'm keen and quite good, really lifted my mood when things were tough in my head. I have a good job as a chef and I can enjoy friends and going out. But I still miss Rory all the time and I know that's it because I don't believe in life after death. But I no longer feel guilty, as I did, that I wasn't the one to die. ∎

KEEPING A FRIEND IN MIND

Laura, 19, saw a dear friend die in a few days from a strain of MRSA. Grieving with his friends helped her deal with the loss.

Chris was a friend I had grown up with since I was very young. We went to the same school and had the same friends. He was always active and good fun, then one day he got what seemed like flu. He complained of feeling droopy and not well, although nobody took it seriously at first. When he was feeling just as bad by the end of the week my mother was worried and she went to see him. While she was there he started shaking and she got him to hospital.

In hospital

Nobody seemed to know what it was. When some friends and I went to visit him on Saturday, the hospital was trying different treatments. We spent Sunday with him too, and by this time he wasn't responding to any treatment and the hospital had nothing more they could do. We all just sat with him and at 7 pm the hospital switched off his life support.

"I'd say to others going through something similar, remember that others probably are minding as much as you are."

Disbelief

At first nobody could say what it was but then they said it was MRSA. It was a horrific shock. I really couldn't believe this dear, close friend was dead. Just like that. And that is how it was for a long time. Everything reminded me of him. I just couldn't accept that Chris and I would never do all the things we had planned.

Leaning on friends

It helped having the group of friends to talk to and we were very tight for quite a while afterwards. We would go to Chris's house a lot and see his mum. We tried to keep the spirit of him alive and she has said how much that helped.

We went on talking about him all the time and it helped to feel we all cared so much. But then the group seemed to drift apart and I had the feeling that for them it was over. Nobody seemed to think about Chris any more. That really upset me so one day I said well I still cared a lot and immediately everyone said they felt the same. I suppose you can't go on talking about it all the time and I'd say to others going through something similar, remember that others probably are minding as much as you are.

Not forgotten

It's 18 months since he died and I'm at university now. It hits me sometimes that Chris would have been too. I have felt guilty at times about enjoying myself but I realise now you shouldn't feel bad about that because it doesn't mean you have forgotten all about the person.

The group still meets up in the holidays and we talk about Chris and remember what a great person he was. ∎

LEANING ON FRIENDS

When a friend dies, it can really help to keep in touch with others in the friendship group. Together you can talk about the dead person naturally, without having to explain everything as you would to a person who never knew them. You can remember the good times, and the bad. Talking over the period leading up to the death can help to come to terms with what happened during a serious illness. If the death was sudden, talking about it can also help everyone cope. Even if you drift apart over time, arranging to meet once a year can help to keep the person's memory alive.

CARING FOR MY MOTHER

Amelia* had a very close relationship with her mother and cared for her at home when she was dying. Amelia feels this has helped her cope.
*Not her real name

Q How was your relationship with your mother?

I was horrible to her in adolescence, but once I had got past this stage things were fantastic and very close. I could talk to her about everything from intellectual to emotional matters. I remember going on my gap year and missing her so much.

Q When did she become ill?

When we went on holiday to Cyprus four years ago she had a lot of pain in her left hip. We assumed it was the beginning of arthritis. The doctor was concerned and sent her for

"I could talk to [my mother] about everything..."

tests and these showed up cancer in the bones and a mammoth tumour on her lungs. My mother was given six months but in fact she lived for two and a half years.

Q How much did this news change your life?

Completely. I had to face Mum being terminally ill. I had been planning to go to America for a year as part of my degree course but I changed my degree to be in the UK. Mum began her chemotherapy and it made her violently unwell. So my focus became keeping Mum as well as possible and alive.

"As a family we never talked about what would happen in the future."

Q What happened then?

I worried about her a lot in a way I never had before. But her strong spirit helped. For instance when her hair started to fall out she was really cool with it which meant my elder sister and my dad and I could laugh with her and call her Baldy. As a family we never talked about what would happen in the future. She was part of that: so generous in coping with her cancer and talking about it reasonably. She was a guinea-pig for a drug, which decreased her tumour by 50% and we were lucky because this prolonged her life.

Q Were your friends a help?

Some were truly helpful, and the situation separated them from friends going, "Oh my God I have to write an essay," while you are thinking, "I have to deal with my mother dying." ▶

CANCER

There are about 200 different types of cancer, including cancer of the blood, of the skin, of the lungs or in the bone. While it is difficult to treat some types of cancer, doctors can treat others much more successfully. Unlike the people mentioned in this book, many people survive cancer and go on to live for many more years.

HOW DOES CANCER START?
Our bodies are made up of millions of cells, most of which are programmed to divide and multiply when necessary for growth or repair. However, sometimes a cell will become damaged and will begin to multiply in an uncontrolled way. This will form a clump of cells called a tumour. Some tumours are benign (harmless), others are cancerous. If left unchecked, a cancerous tumour will grow and spread around the body, threatening life.

Q Did your mother know how you were feeling?

I talked to her about it a lot. I would tell her I was scared and she would say like "come on darling, got to keep going." Then in the summer of 2005 Mum had a secondary growth in her brain diagnosed. And the terrible thing was I felt furious with this headstrong, wonderful woman for being ill.

Q So how did you deal with things at this stage?

I quit law school, which I had just started, after four weeks, when my mother was clearly spiralling downhill. I knew she wanted to be at home when she died and I wanted to make that possible so I chose to take on caring for her.

Q What did that involve?

We got medical care because she was becoming bed-ridden. I'd make her eat porridge, which I believe kept her going. She had a wheelchair and I took her out. There were days when I would sprawl my body over hers and sob my eyes out. She would rub the back of my neck with her hand. But it was a peaceful time with her room full of scented candles. She was in nappies by the end and nurses taught me to change them and I would get in the shower with her while Dad would wash her down. I did things I never imagined, like wiping her private parts.

"I'd make her eat porridge, which I believe kept her going."

Did doing this help you?

I felt it was the last thing I could do for her and I drew on strength I didn't know I had. I think my grieving took place during these six months before she died. But after the funeral it got worse. I wanted Mum to be talked about and remembered all the time but of course that wasn't happening.

How did you look after yourself?

I knew I must be kind and gentle with myself. I watched lots of DVDs and just did what I felt like. That included going out and having fun with friends.

I didn't try to rush anything. And slowly, slowly it became possible to see happy things in life; small good things and that life does go on.

How do you see the future now?

I am a very positive person and I think having been with my family doing all we possibly could for my mother was very important. There's nothing left that I feel I should have said to her. I've been offered lots of help but I don't feel I need it just now. If in time I get depressed and stuck I may well seek help. Just now I can imagine having a career, getting married, having children and although it is incredibly sad to think Mum won't be there, I can feel optimistic. ∎

HOLDING ON TO MEMORIES

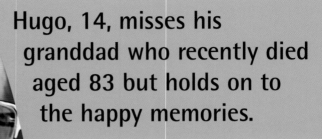

Hugo, 14, misses his granddad who recently died aged 83 but holds on to the happy memories.

As a family we visited my grandparents in the country several times a year and I would go during school holidays. My granddad and I used to go for long walks; he organised Easter Egg hunts and he was always introducing me to his hobbies – we carved wooden things in his workshop.

As I grew older I enjoyed his very opinionated way of talking and I liked his stories. Some people complained he droned on about the Second World War and India, but I enjoyed it. He and my grandma had a holiday in France with us all and that was very happy.

Sudden death

I hadn't had any experience of people dying and although Granddad was quite old I didn't think about him dying as he seemed very healthy. When he did die it wasn't natural causes. I was in France with my family

" ... although Granddad
was quite old I didn't think
about him dying..."

the days before New Year. We got a phone call from my uncle in England. He had been with my grandparents. He told us my Granddad had had an accident and was in a coma. He had gone shopping on Boxing Day and slipped on ice. He fell and cracked his head open.

FUNERALS

After someone dies, most people organise a funeral so that everyone who knew the dead person can gather together to pay their respects and say a final goodbye. Funerals can be a gathering of people in a chosen place, or a religious service in a church, temple, mosque or synagogue. They can be led by a religious person or a non-religious person, or can be a shared experience where people take turns to speak about the dead person's life, say poems or play music. A religious funeral usually follows a set service that can include a eulogy (a spoken tribute to the dead person), prayers and communal hymn-singing. Religious funerals can also include special music, poems or readings.

After the funeral, the burial or cremation takes place. The dead person, inside a coffin, is either buried in the ground or cremated (burnt) at a crematorium. The ashes are usually scattered or buried at a later date.

My feelings then were real sadness for my dad because I hadn't seen him so upset before and I suppose it is the people closest to you who preoccupy you most. Then we heard Granddad would be in a vegetative state if he came out of the coma. Grandma talked with all the relatives and everyone agreed it would be best not to keep him alive.

At the funeral it hit me I would never see him again. I was sad but most concerned with helping my mother comfort my father. It was at the memorial service that I cried. People read out very moving things they had written or poems and a lot of people were crying.

Afterwards I felt sad but I thought a lot about the good things we had done together and how he had loved me. And I saw that there was no point bringing myself down. It wouldn't help anyone. I don't think Granddad would have wanted me to go on mourning.

Still sad

But I do miss him. I miss the conversations we used to have, and when I went to see my Grandma who was mourning, it brought back the sad feelings.

I suppose I have had to face the fact that death happens to people you care for and I hope that has given me a bit of maturity for the next time. I would say to other kids that finding someone to talk to is very important. And you have to accept that feeling sad is part of life and it's how it will be at times. ■

COPING WITH A TRAGIC DEATH

Maya lost her father when she was 13 and her mother died in an horrific road accident eight months ago.

Q Did you grow up with both parents?

My father died when I was 13, but I had never known him as the dynamic creative writer he was and whom my mother had adored. He got meningitis when she was pregnant with me and his whole personality changed. He rejected me a great deal and I became a very spiky, anxious child. Even so it was a loss when he died and then more so when I read diaries of my mother, Emma – I always called her that – and later she told me about Raj, my father. I saw the enormous creativity he had had and the relationship full of joy that she had with him.

"My father died when I was 13, but I had never known him as the dynamic creative writer he was and whom my mother had adored."

Q How did your mother cope?

She was an incredibly strong woman. She and my father had separated and she had a new partner, Reg. I remember him saying to my mother Emma, "You are always so happy and it's so great to come home to." I had reached a point with her as a young adult where I appreciated her and she appreciated me and we were very similar in many ways. We had big conversations. I was aware of feeling very contented and that life was good.

Q Then that changed?

On December 21st 2006 the police came to the door to tell us Emma had had a terrible accident with a vehicle. We went straight to where it had happened and before anyone official had the chance to tell us a journalist was there saying, "Oh yeah it was a cement mixer that killed her." Being told in that way was just so awful and the journalist was really excited to have the family there and kept offering us her card.

Emma had been on her bicycle on her way to work. She was a very careful cyclist and was wearing her helmet and reflective jacket. It was at a three-way road junction near King's Cross [in London] and Emma had stopped at traffic lights. The two-tonne cement mixer had also stopped there. The guy in the cab of the mixer was picking up some documents from the pocket of his cab – I saw it all on CCTV footage – and probably not concentrating. But with three mirrors and no blind spot he had no excuse for not seeing her. The lights changed and she turned left. The mixer did the same and it was then that she got caught in its wheels. It seems people started beeping and, all apart from one, said in evidence that they thought he hadn't seen Emma. The vehicle just went over her with the back wheels and did not stop. It was the most brutal way to die. ▶

"The guy in the cab of the mixer was picking up some documents from the pocket of his cab — I saw it all on CCTV footage — and probably not concentrating."

Q How do you begin to cope with such a terrible death?

Worst of all was learning that the cement-mixer driver had gone on honeymoon and the police hadn't even interviewed him. It took a while for the driver to be charged and even then it was only for driving without due care and attention, which is a minor offence. But this wasn't an accident, my mother was killed as I see it. My sister cried a lot, her partner drank and I was in pieces. I rang everybody I could because I was frantic. We were in hell.

Q It is eight months since it happened – how are you coping now?

I think I've been strong but I have this great knot of sadness. I believe a good bereavement counsellor could have helped but that didn't happen. I am very emotionally detached from almost everyone. When you meet people and tell them what happened it's like you've launched a grenade and they don't know what to do. People are so conscious of getting things wrong and don't know what to say. I wish they'd realise there's nothing right to say. The wrong thing has happened. Yet people saying anything at all and the letters make a big difference. It mattered that so many people came to the funeral.

"I am very emotionally detached from almost everyone."

> "... the sadness is really setting in now. Emma was the person I cared most about in the world."

However I am getting on with life. I work. I am being competent and I play a role. But the sadness is really setting in now. Emma was the person I cared most about in the world. She was the person I needed for 22 years and I'm having a million recollections.

 ## How does time ahead look?

I don't want to be a different person because of this. I want to maintain the strength Emma had given me. But it is made more difficult by the fact that the court found the driver guilty of driving without due care and attention, fined him £250 and allowed him to keep his licence even though he admits he didn't even double check his mirror. That's the price of my mother's life. Grieving is not easy when you see such injustice and feel so impotent. ∎

BEREAVEMENT COUNSELLING

If talking to friends or family isn't working, it might be a help to talk to a trained bereavement counsellor. These specialists receive training in talking to people who have lost someone close to them. They have learnt how to talk to bereaved people, or simply listen to them, and can help them come through grief. They are skilled in helping people deal with traumatic deaths caused by violent actions or accidents. They may also be able to give practical advice on money matters and legal situations that arise when someone dies. Cruse Bereavement Care (see page 31) should be able to give advice on local bereavement counsellors.

HEARING FROM ABROAD

David heard, while trekking in Nepal, that his very close friend had died suddenly of meningitis.

Q How close were you and Eddie?

We met at secondary school and became real soul mates. We had lots of fun bantering, swapping jokes, having a beer together. I spent quite a lot of time with him at his home. When we left school we kept a lot of contact.

Q But you were not around when he became fatally ill?

It was my gap year and I was trekking in Nepal with another good friend from our comprehensive school. I remember the evening before we went having a few beers with Eddie and he was telling silly jokes and wishing me well. But we didn't see the need to keep in touch while I was away. We knew it would be just the same when I got back and we met up.

Q So how did you find out what happened?

My friend and I had been having a great time and we were just at the end of our time in Nepal, ready to

> "I plucked a rhododendron [flower] and I went out in a boat and chucked it into the lake. It felt very symbolic."

head for Vietnam. I got a phone message from Mum asking me to call home. She told me Eddie had gone to bed with aches and pains and never recovered. It was meningitis and he died within 12 hours.

 ## How did the news affect you?

I was absolutely devastated. The immediate effect was physical. I couldn't walk. I cried a lot. My friendship with Eddie had been based on the idea that we were invincible, immortal. I phoned his dad to say I'd come home and he told me he'd kick my ass if I did. That I should go on with the trip because Eddie would have wanted it. So I did.

 ## How easy was it to do this?

In fact my friend and I went a bit wild. I thought Eddie would have loved that. My friend comforted me and because he was as close as Eddie there wasn't a problem with him feeling less important. We went together to Pokrha and did a memorial ritual for Eddie. I plucked a rhododendron [flower] and I went out in a boat and chucked it into the lake. It felt very symbolic. I then wrote a long speech for Eddie's funeral and writing down my feelings was very helpful. I sent it to my mum to read out.

 ## Did you feel a bit lost after this?

Ironically my friend got a stomach complaint and I had to look after him which gave me a sense of purpose.

We then spent three months in Vietnam travelling around on motorbikes, so I had a lot of time with my thoughts and it enabled me to process the stuff around Eddie. That was valuable because it meant I was in the right state to make new friends, have a laugh, enjoy the experiences we were having. Now and again there was a little cry.

 ## How was it when you got back to the UK?

That was harder. I went to see his dad straight away and he was in a bad state. And I missed Eddie more now that I was home. I went to the last pub we drank in but I didn't feel the need to talk about it to friends. In my head was the way Eddie would have talked to me. He'd be saying, "Come on, get on with it. I've only died."

 ## Does the grief go on?

I have a lot of very fond memories but I'm not stuck with grief. I feel I've acknowledged how important he was and that makes it possible to get on with living. ∎

FEELING BETRAYED

Charlie felt betrayed by her close uncle's death and did not know how to deal with the grief.

I was named after my uncle. He was posh and scary but also very warm and lovely, and always treated me as a grown-up whom he enjoyed talking to. He had no daughter and I think that was what I represented to him. He was an Anglo-Saxon historian at Oxford University and always took a great interest in my education. I'm sure it was partly because of him that I got into Trinity College at Oxford. And I did Anglo-Saxon in my first year.

It was during this year that Mum told me he had had an affair with a student close to my age, which upset me. There was a lot of family anger at him. It was just before his 50th birthday and he had what I suppose is a mid-life crisis. His marriage ended. He was in trouble at Oxford and he was drinking a lot.

But then he stopped drinking and he came back to being the man I loved. He had a new partner and he started coming to visit us which was wonderful.

"Mum told me he had had an affair with a student close to my age, which upset me."

28

I was studying *Paradise Lost* and he told me he had played the part of Satan in a school production of the poem. That was the last time I saw him.

I remember Dad telling me my uncle had collapsed after drinking and not been found for three weeks. His body was decomposed.

Aftermath

I went to the flat to support his two sons who were there. The body was gone but my uncle's hair had fallen out and was in the room; there were flies everywhere. I found myself thinking later about how I could have saved him.

I went back to university and it was a very bad time. I had broken up with my boyfriend. I felt my friends were scared I would pour emotion all over them. I tried getting back with my boyfriend but after a week he said he couldn't deal with my being so upset. It seemed there was nobody who could accept my being so sad.

> "I felt my friends were scared I would pour emotion all over them."

Breaking down

The world felt a very harsh place. I cried and cried. I didn't sleep at nights. I was enormously stressed. I started thinking I didn't care about anyone.

I had been given three presentations to do on the same day at university. I went in to my tutor and sat in front of her and couldn't remember anything. She understood how serious it was and got on the phone to the counsellor and said she had an emergency case. The counsellor was really good.

LOOKING AFTER YOURSELF

Whilst coping with grief, it is important to look after your body, however unimportant it might seem. Grief makes your immune system not work as well so you are vulnerable to infections. Remember to eat plenty of fruit and vegetables and to keep drinking water, even if you don't feel like eating or drinking. Keep clean and take some gentle exercise. Try not to shut yourself away from people but make some social plans and keep to them. Go at your own pace though – don't feel pressurised by others to 'get over' your grief.

Moving on

After this I was able to tell friends who were kinder than I had imagined, about what I had seen in my uncle's room, and that helped a lot. I could study again and it seemed I was doing it for my uncle. In a way I had felt betrayed by him dying, but when I took my finals and got a first [class degree] I felt this was his legacy and it was possible to go forward. ■

GLOSSARY

adolescence
The state of development that someone is in between puberty and adulthood.

Anglo-Saxon historian
Someone who studies the Anglo-Saxons – a group of tribes originating from Germany who achieved dominance in southern Britain from the mid-5th century to the mid-11th century, forming the earliest basis for the modern English nation, language and culture.

arthritis
Inflammation of the joints which causes pain, swelling and stiffness.

CCTV
Closed Circuit Television. Cameras used to monitor city centres and other places 24 hours a day.

chemotheraphy
Treatment with drugs to destroy cancer cells. Chemotherapy is often used with surgery or radiation to treat cancer when the cancer has spread, when it has come back (recurred), or when there is a strong chance that it could recur.

decompose
To rot or decay.

gap year
A 12-month period, usually after the end of secondary school and prior to starting at university, when a young person travels or works abroad.

grenade
A small explosive device, usually hand thrown.

hysterical
Excessive or uncontrollable emotion.

legacy
Something handed down or inherited from generation to generation.

lethargic
When you feel drowsy and don't feel like doing much.

melancholy
A feeling of thoughtful sadness.

meningitis
An infection of the lining of the brain. If bacterial meningitis is not treated within hours, it can lead to death or permanent brain injury.

mourning
A state of sorrow over the death or departure of a loved one.

MRSA
(Methicillin Resistant Staphylococcus Aureus.) Staphylococcus Aureus is a common bug found in the nose, skin, etc of healthy people. Some strains of Staphylococcus Aureus are resistant to the antibiotic Methicillin and other antibiotics. They are harder to treat and cause more problems and in the worst cases can kill people.

plethora
A lot of something.

surreal
When something feels like a dream.

tumour
This term describes any growth of tissue forming an abnormal mass. Cells of a benign tumour will not spread and will not cause cancer. Cells of a malignant tumour can spread through the body and cause cancer.

FURTHER INFORMATION

ORGANISATIONS & HELPLINES

Careline
Tel: 0845 122 8622
Web: www.carelineuk.org
Telephone counselling for people of any age, on any issue.

Child Bereavement Trust
Tel: 01494 446648
Web: www.childbereavement.org.uk
Web: www.rd4u.org.uk
They recommend books and DVDs and publish leaflets to help adults understand bereaved childrens' feelings. They also have a Youth Involvement Project – RD4U – run by a group of 16-25 year-olds who have experienced bereavement, and who come from diverse backgrounds, cultures and religions.

ChildLine
Free helpline: 0800 1111
Web: www.childline.org.uk
Telephone counselling for any child with any problem.

Cruse Bereavement Care
Young Person's freephone: 0808 808 1677
Web: www.crusebereavementcare.org.uk/
Cruse Bereavement Care exists to promote the well-being of bereaved people and to enable anyone bereaved by death to understand their grief and cope with their loss. The organisation provides counselling and support. It offers information, advice, education and training services.

Get Connected
Free helpline: 0808 808 4994
Web: www.getconnected.org.uk
Helpline for young people.

Samaritans
Tel: 08457 90 90 90
Web: www.samaritans.org.uk
Support for anyone in crisis.

There4me
Web: www.there4me.com
Email support service for young people between 12-16 years.

Youth Access
Helpline: 020 8896 3675
Web: www.youthaccess.org.uk
Counselling services for young people aged 12–25 years.

Youth2Youth
Web: www.youth2youth.co.uk
Email and telephone support, run by young volunteers for under 19s.

Winston's Wish
Helpline: 08452 03 04 05
General enquiries: 01242 515157
Web: www.winstonswish.org.uk
A charity that offers support to young people who have experienced bereavement.

FURTHER WEBSITES

www.bbc.co.uk/relationships/coping_with_grief/bereavement
A very useful site on coping with bereavement.

www.youngminds.org.uk
The young people's mental health charity.

www.thesite.org
Articles on young people's issues including health and wellbeing.

AUSTRALIA/NEW ZEALAND

www.kidshelp.com.au
Free helpline: 1800 55 1800
Telephone and online counselling for young people under 25.

www.youthline.co.nz
Support for young people in New Zealand.

INDEX

accidental death, 21, 22, 23-24, 25

anger 4, 5, 11, 12, 18, 24-25

bereavement,
common reactions to 4-5

betrayal 28-29

cancer 6-7, 10-11, 16-17, 30

chemotherapy 17, 30

Child Bereavement Trust 6, 31

counsellors 11, 12, 29, 31
bereavement 24, 25, 31

Cruse Bereavement Care 25, 31

denial 4, 5, 11

depression 5, 8, 11-12, 19

friends, leaning on 14-15, 27

funerals 8, 18, 21, 24, 27

grief, process of 12

guilt 4, 5, 6-9, 12, 13, 15

loss,
of a brother 4, 10-13
of a friend 4, 14-15, 26-27
of a granddad 4, 20-21
of a mother 4, 6-9, 16-19, 22-25
of an uncle 4, 28-29

memories 5, 15, 20, 21, 27

meningitis 22, 26, 27, 30

MRSA 14, 15, 30

organisations,
child bereavement 5, 31

sadness 7, 11, 12, 19, 21, 24, 25, 29, 30

shock 7, 11, 27

sport 9, 13

TALKING POINTS

The interviews in this book may provoke a range of reactions: shock, sympathy, empathy, sadness. As many of the interviewees found, talking can help you to sort out your emotions. If you wish to talk about the interviews here are some questions to get you started:

Liana's story - page 6
Why do you think guilt is a common feeling for people who have lost a loved one? What things could Liana do to help her to stop feeling so guilty?

Dan's story - page 10
What signs were there that Dan was depressed? Dan says sport helped him. What other practical things might help with bereavement?

Laura's story - page 14
How does the way someone dies - for example suddenly or over a long period - affect those who are left behind? Why does leaning on friends help with the grieving process?

Amelia's story - page 16
How do you think helping to care for her mother helped Amelia later on? Should families generally put their lives 'on hold' in such situations?

Hugo's story - page 20
Is it necessarily easier to accept the death of an elderly person do you think? How important are funerals in the grieving process?

Maya's story - page 22
Do you think a stronger punishment for the driver would help Maya? Do you agree that her mother was killed?

David's story - page 26
David hears about the death of his friend Eddie from abroad and he decides to miss the funeral as this is what Eddie would have wanted. What would you do in a similar situation?

Charlie's story - page 28
Why do you think people are sometimes afraid to talk to a friend about their grief?

These are the lists of contents for each title in *Talking About Myself*:

Depression
What is depression? • All alone • Love's lost • Drug-taking depression • Accepting the past • Years of depression • Managing meltdown - bipolar disorder • Pushy parent • Attempted suicide

Eating Disorders
What are eating disorders? • Recovering anorexic • Fighting bulimia • Reaction to bullying - male anorexia • Dangerous images • Symptom of depression • From obese to bulimic • Fighting obesity • Feeling good at last

Losing a loved one
Coping with loss • Living with guilt • Losing a brother • Keeping a friend in mind • Caring for my mother • Holding on to memories - losing a granddad • Coping with a tragic death • Hearing from abroad • Feeling betrayed

My family
What is a family? • Dealing with divorce • When my parents split up • Father and son difficulties • Keeping the peace • Difficult at any age • Meeting my father for the first time • Care and adoption • Caring for my mother

Racism
What is racism? • Trying to belong - a Muslim's story • Culture clash • Being the outsider • Anti-Semitic attack • Bullied by other Muslims • Breaking down racism • Not allowed to mix • Growing up with racism

Relationships & Sex
First relationhips • Sleeping around • Sex without attachment • Glad to be gay • Dealing with homophobia • Losing my relationships confidence • Becoming a single parent • Young father • Childhood abuse